This Book Belongs to:

_____

Merry Christmas!

What presents do you hope Santa brings on his motorcycle?

What is the dogs name?

Draw what is in the present boxes.

Draw your favorite Christmas moment

Start at the north pole. Get through the maze to deliver presents.

Draw a snowball fight

Nice List   Naughty List

Decorate Santa's Workshop

Draw and color what you think Santa's workshop looks like. Add elves, toys, and magical decorations!

Design Your Own Ugly Christmas Sweater

Create the craziest, most colorful Christmas sweater design. Don't forget the festive patterns and quirky decorations!

Draw and color Santa's reindeer playing games or having a snowball fight. Give each reindeer a unique personality!

Design and color your own cozy Christmas village. Include houses, a town square, and cheerful villagers celebrating.

Create a scene of singing animals or kids caroling in the snow. Add music notes and lyrics for a festive touch!

Draw and list what your are grateful for this Christmas season.

Made in United States
Troutdale, OR
12/19/2023

16133499R00015